PICKLES FOR PAPAW

Kristin G Bridges

Illustrated by Keaton Clulow

Copyright © 2020 Kristin Bridges
All rights reserved.

No part of this publication in print or in electronic format may be reproduced, stored in a retrieval system, or transmitted in any form or by any means, electronic, mechanical, photocopying, recording, or otherwise, without the prior written permission of the publisher.

This is a work of fiction. Names, characters, organizations, places, events, and incidents are either the products of the author's imagination or are used fictitiously. Any resemblance to actual persons, living or dead, or actual events is purely coincidental.

Illustrations by Keaton Clulow

ISBN: 978-1-64704-252-3 (hardback)
ISBN: 978-1-64704-238-7 (paperback)
ISBN: 978-1-64704-239-4 (eBook)

*To Allison,
Enjoy!
Kristin Britt*

For my children, grandchildren, and generations to come. May they know and appreciate the simple things in life.

In loving memory of my grandparents: "Poppin," who loved my homemade pickles, and "Gromin," whose collection of canning jars inspired the garden and this book.

This is our Papaw. He grew up on a farm.
He loves fresh vegetables and fruit.

One summer, our Mom decided
we should plant a garden.

We tilled the soil.

We planted seeds and baby plants.

We planted tomatoes, corn, and squash.

We planted green beans, peppers, onions...

...pumpkins and cucumbers.

We watered the garden and
we pulled the weeds.

The seeds grew into baby plants.

All the plants grew and grew.

The plants made lots of vegetables.

Mom showed us how to save the vegetables in jars so we could enjoy them all winter.

We canned beans and tomatoes, and we froze squash and pumpkins.

Mom found an old pickle recipe from Grandma.

We helped Mom slice cucumbers and onions.

She cooked them in a big pot with vinegar, sugar, and spices.

We sealed them all up in jars.

We gave Papaw two jars of pickles.

He loves our pickles,
so we keep bringing him more . . .

...until next Spring, when we will plant
a new garden to make more pickles for Papaw.

Country Preacher's Kid Bread & Butter Pickles

Tips: I use cucumbers that are no more than 1 to 1 ½ inches in diameter and cut them to a little over ⅛-inch-thick slices using the serrated blade on my mandolin, but they can be sliced with a knife as well.

Use 1 pint canning jars with regular size lids. Be sure to boil all canning supplies for 10 minutes before using to ensure they are sanitary. I use a ladle and canning funnel to fill the jars. Be sure to wipe the edge with a clean, damp paper towel to avoid sticking. You know the jars are sealed correctly when you hear the lid pop!

Ingredients:

- 1-gallon sliced cucumbers (about 9 medium-sized cucumbers)
- 3 medium yellow onions, sliced thin
- ½ cup kosher or coarse sea salt
- Crushed ice
- 5 cups sugar
- ½ tsp. turmeric
- 2 Tbsp. mustard seed
- 1 Tbsp. celery seed
- 3 cups white vinegar

Yield: about 5 pints

Directions:

Place cucumbers, onions, and salt in a large pot and gently stir together. Add enough crushed ice to cover the top. Let sit for 3 hours. Drain. Do not rinse.

In a medium bowl, combine sugar, turmeric, mustard seed, celery seed, and vinegar. Pour over the cucumbers and onions and heat to a boil, gently stirring occasionally for even cooking. Shut off the heat.

Put the pickle mixture into hot canning jars, filling to about ½ inch below top and seal the lids to finger tight. Let sit on counter until the lids pop.

Properly sealed jars will keep for about a year in the pantry. If a jar doesn't seal or is only partially full, place in refrigerator for use immediately as you would any open jar of pickles.

CPSIA information can be obtained
at www.ICGtesting.com
Printed in the USA
LVHW071127201020
669267LV00010B/141